An Adult Guide
to the Orchestra

This edition is published by Darkhorse Books, a division of Darkhorse Theater, inc.

Darkhorse Books
4610 Charlotte Ave.
Nashville, TN 37209
Visit us online at DarkhorseBooksOnline.com

FIRST EDITION
AUGUST, 2011

a 1 a 2 a 1 2 3 4

ISBN 978-0615526782
ISBN 0615526780

SHELDON KURLAND, a Juilliard-trained violinist, taught music at Cornell University and Peabody College, where his specialty was inventing musical history facts upon which his students were eventually tested.

As a young man, he won the Major Bowes Amateur Radio Hour before turning pro later in life with the Tulsa Symphony Orchestra, where he was Assistant Concertmaster, much to his chagrin. For a brief while, he carried an iron clarinet in the 5th Armored Division Band. He also played in the Cornell University Trio, the Cumberland Trio, and to his own surprise, he played once with the Nashville Symphony Orchestra.

After leaving the college professor business, he went into the recording industry full-time, playing with a wide variety of artists, from Elvis Presley and Johnny Cash, to Bob Dylan and Dolly Parton. He had cameo appearances in the films <u>Wild Wild West</u> and <u>Existo</u> and toured with Neil Young. His hope was always to become a professional baseball player but he ended up with more lifetime hits than Pete Rose.

In his spare time, Shelly was a dedicated writer, turning out numerous short stories, memoirs, and a play, <u>The Bluebird Cafe</u> as well as this book. Sheldon Kurland died in 2010, taking him halfway to his goal of a posthumous Pulitzer.

JANET SWANSON, illustrator, is a well-known portrait artist and sculptor, trained at the Philadelphia Museum School of Industrial Art. Her work is seen in many homes and galleries. She lives on Cape Cod.

Typical Orchestra Setup

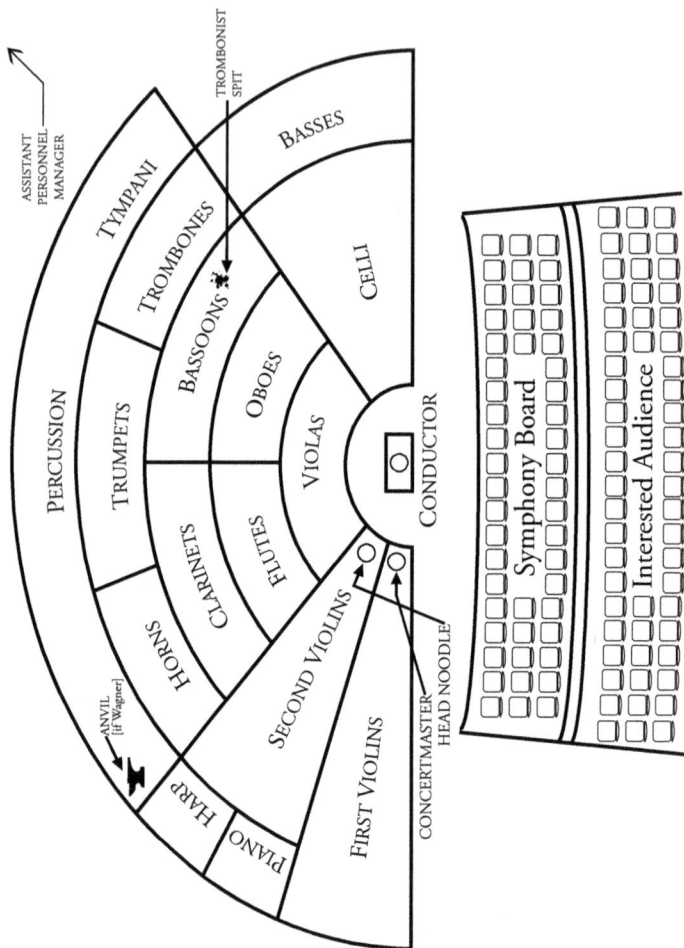

ASSISTANT PERSONNEL MANAGER

TROMBONIST SPIT

BASSES

TYMPANI

TROMBONES

CELLI

PERCUSSION

TRUMPETS

BASSOONS

OBOES

VIOLAS

CONDUCTOR

CLARINETS

FLUTES

HORNS

SECOND VIOLINS

ANVIL [if Wagner]

HARP

PIANO

FIRST VIOLINS

CONCERTMASTER HEAD NOODLE

Symphony Board

Interested Audience

GRAPHIC © BEN KURLAND

CONTENTS

An Adult Guide to the Orchestra

Sheldon Kurland

There they are. Those seventy or ninety or two hundred (if it's the movies) happy members of the symphony. Such ensemble, such beauty, such romance.

An Adult Guide to the Orchestra

Part One
The Strings

The most important thing in a string player's life is where he sits. From the moment he gets to play his first student orchestra rehearsal he learns that his abilities are judged by the chair assigned. First chair outside is the star. Last chair inside at the back of the section is pathetic. The closer he is to the conductor, the better he feels. If he sits in the eighth chair he is clearly worse than the person in the seventh chair. It is out there for all to see. On the other hand he feels vastly superior to everyone behind him. He will do anything in order to move up with the possible exception of practicing. He knows that getting moved back is politics and moving forward is talent. This cutthroat system exists in all the string sections but seems to be exceptionally acute in the violins. Playing first violin is all important. Second fiddlers spend their lives in analysis if they can afford it.

Two violinists always share one stand and one piece of music. It is very important to be the outside player who is closest to the audience. It is traditional that the inside player gets to do the dirty work like turning the pages. After all, the outsider is ranked higher in ability so if the insider does not play some of the music while turning, it will do the performance no harm. The inside man is also expected to bring the pencil and let his stand partner have the better view of the music and choose the height of the stand. Even though the inside player knows that he has been ranked higher than everyone behind him, this inferior position on the stand is humiliating. It does not make for lifelong friendships.

Violin students spend many hours holding up their instruments with their left shoulders. Then they haul heavy violin cases full of junk to lessons and rehearsals with their right arms. Consequently you can always tell violinists or violists by their shape. They look like oil derrick pumps stopped in weird positions. Add to that the ugly red marks under their chins, and you don't have to be Sherlock Holmes to spot one. Glamourous women violinists have four long, beautiful, painted fingernails, three on the right hand and one on the left thumb. The rest are stubs, usually bitten off during rehearsals. But that's just the outer beauty.

The ranges of the first and second violins are the same. The violin starts at G below middle C going up about four octaves or more depending on how high you can stand it. Stopping each string (putting your finger down on it) half the length raises the pitch one octave. Stopping half of what is left brings you up another octave. Half of that remaining part will give you another octave and so on. Except for the pitches getting closer and closer on the string to a point where your fingers will not fit, there is theoretically no limit to how high you can go, especially if you don't care what it sounds like.

The first violins get to use the entire four octaves while the seconds usually are restricted to the bottom two. Violins and flutes are the sopranos of the orchestra when it comes to range. Double bass cases filled with lead are the sopranos of the orchestra when it comes to weight.

In <u>The Ascending Lark</u> by Ralph Vaughan Williams for Violin and Orchestra, the solo violinist plays in the highest stratospheres of the instrument. Sometimes at that altitude both the violinist and the bird lay an egg.

THIS IS A SERIOUS WARNING. When you meet a violinist on the street, never ask him, "What have you got in there, a machine gun?" It may be the millionth time he has heard it that month and he will kill you.

The First Violin Section

The first violins sit on the outer edge of the stage on the left. This allows them to look for friends and family (a few have those). This, of course, drives the assistant personnel manager crazy. The main duty of the assistant personnel manager is to sit through rehearsals and concerts and spot breaches in decorum, no matter how slight. To be an assistant personnel manager one must be forty-two years old, have spent no more than one year in a music education program in a college in Mississippi and be a virgin. Major offenses could be a glimpse of stocking or poor page turning. When an assistant personnel manager becomes forty-three years old and has sufficient experience in nit-picking, he can be appointed full personnel manager. This allows him to refuse time off to an orchestra player whose entire family has just contracted the plague.

The large symphony uses eighteen firsts. The first, first violin is called the concertmaster. At concerts he gets to arrive on the stage after all the rest of the orchestra is seated. No one knows why he does this, but it is expected. Maybe his reward for making it to number one is not having to spend too much time with the assistant concertmaster who is trying to get his job. The concertmaster also gets to point at an oboe player. In return the oboist makes a funny sound. All the members of the orchestra will then pretend that they heard a tuning note. This will cause them to start practicing the music for the first time. First violinists will play the show-off parts of concertos. The assistant personnel manager will become irate.

THE SECOND VIOLIN SECTION

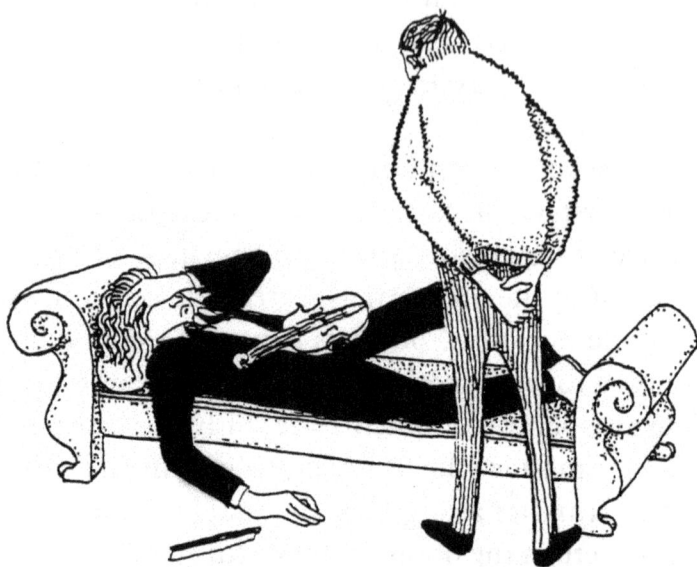

Being a second fiddle is very painful. The section is tucked behind the first violins with the hope that no one will see what they are doing. The important parts in all music are the top or treble voice (the melody) and the bottom notes in the bass line. Second violins play some peculiar inner voice, and only a foolhardy composer would let them touch the melody. Some ask, "Is the person who takes the exalted position of first chair in the seconds better that the last chair first?" First chair of the seconds is as important as being the head noodle in a pasta salad.

There are sixteen second violin players. As the distance to the conductor grows and the quality of the playing diminishes, the difference between the speed of light and that of sound takes over. The violinist whose ambition was to be a soloist before he became a member of an orchestra now tries desperately not to be one. In the back of the section, not playing by yourself becomes all important. If you sit in the last-chair-second violins and play an inadvertent solo your next chair will be in the state unemployment office. Not making this fatal mistake is accomplished by hardly playing at all. You just use the middle inch of the bow which is a shame because you paid for all of that horse hair and wood. But just in case you might be heard anyway, do not watch the conductor even for an instant. You play a new note only after you are sure the person in front is playing it. Obviously as the note is being passed to the back, the time delay becomes awesome. If you sometimes wonder why it looks like the beat of the conductor seems to have nothing to do with the beat of the orchestra, it is because the beat of the conductor has nothing to do with the beat of the orchestra.

All musicians and golfers think that if they only had better equipment they would be perfect. Second violinist are always on the lookout for magic violins and bows. This allows families of string players to live in hovels while incredibly large payments are being given to greedy instrument dealers. The bow alone can cost tens of thousand of dollars. If the player ever gets close to owning his instrument, the dealer is ready with another, more expensive, great Italian master that will keep the string player in poverty forever. Of course, second violinists sound exactly the same no matter how expensive an instrument they play.

THE CELLO SECTION

Let us skip over the violas for now and go on to the cello section. There are twelve cellists in the full sized orchestra. They get to sit on the edge of the stage on the right hand side of the conductor. The main advantage of being a cellist is you play the National Anthem sitting down.

Cellists are very proud that they are aloof from players who have red rashes on their necks. Of course, they are all horribly bowlegged. In order to maintain their modesty, glamourous women cellists, flashing their three long fingernails (you get one fewer than violinists) buy large air force surplus nylon parachutes, which they dye black. Without any alterations they wear them as concert dresses. It makes them look like gigantic, ruffled volley balls. This is highly approved of by assistant personnel managers.

THIS IS A SERIOUS WARNING. Do not allow any cellist, no matter how great he or she may be, to play in your home. A cello has a pointed steel rod built into the bottom of the instrument. It is used primarily for punching holes in fine Oriental carpeting. Although they claim they have little gadgets for taking care of the problem, all cellist have the weapons and the desire to turn fine maple floors into shredded wheat in about fifteen minutes.

Because of the size of a case, a cellist is forced to buy a full priced ticket for his instrument on an airplane. After carefully strapping the seat belt around the case, sun glasses and a hat are added to make everything look more natural. Some cellists used to pre-order the Kosher meals for their instruments. Now the cellist and his cello are lucky to get peanuts.

The cellists are the most arrogant of the string players, but they should remember that they are also in the musical chair competitive rat race and that howling wolves reside in the best of their instruments. On at least one or two notes (every cello is different) horrible shrieks pop up without warning. Cellists think that by gluing and screwing various voodoo devices into the wood and the bridge they can control it. Only they think so. Add to this the rising cost of a set of silver cello strings that will soon rival that of the Stealth Bomber, they should realize that just not being a violinist doesn't make them perfect.

The Double Bass Section

Behind the celli, and stretching single file to the back of the stage stands the double bass section. They are resplendent with their buzzing, disreputable instruments strung with elevator cables and their messy clothing. Not only do they have to stay upright for The Star Spangled Banner but everything else as well. Tall wooden stools are allowed during rehearsals, but since the major activity of bass players is knocking over these seats with much crashing and banging, the bassists are not entrusted to use them during concerts. However even though the instrument has only one leg, a resourceful player can find ways of balancing himself on the shoulders of the bass in order to take a nap during slow movements.

Because the bass section stands, the audience can see the full outfit required of symphony members. These are the wrong people to represent the orchestra sartorially. Some will wear neither suspenders nor belt but will tie lengths of dirty rope around their pants. A triumph for a bassist is getting through an entire concert wearing a long T shirt stamped with formal clothing. Bass players also go into debt to buy old Italian instruments which they keep in solid steel cases that can only be moved by derricks. They then buy some big, bright yellow thing that's sort of shaped like a bass which they use when working.

Bass players are probably the most lovable of the string players, (which is not saying much) and have many outside interests. Playing in tune is not one of them. It is safe to invite a bassist to your home because his steel spike is encased in rubber. If you ask him to play his good instrument, expect to pay a large moving bill.

THE VIOLA SECTION

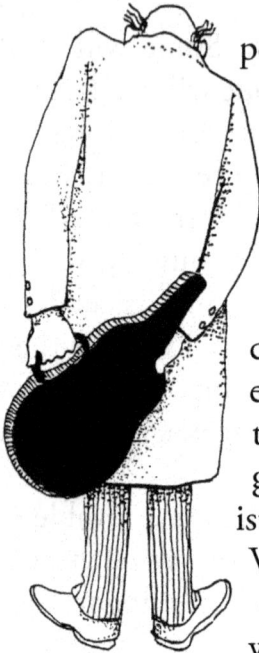

I have postponed as long as possible an analysis of the infected appendage of the orchestra known as the violi. Resented by all, serving a negative musical purpose and costing money, they sit there behind the self satisfied celli, having absolutely no self esteem of their own. None is the right amount. Some try to gain status by marrying violinists. It finishes off the violinists. Virtually all violists are second violin dropouts. I use the word "virtually" in case some violist can prove that he gave up even before the race began and started on the viola. Consequently they have little technique, a horrible sound, and only use vibrato [see Glossary] when nervous.

They alternately play in two different clefs (alto and treble). Music publishers and copyists who are all practical jokers like to switch these clefs in the middle of melodic lines in the most absurd places. This allows the rest of the orchestra an extra ten minute break while viola players try to remember the names of their strings, what the clefs represent and where they should put their fingers.

Viola players are the only people in the orchestra who are seated so that their sound is projected away from the audience to the back of the stage with the hope that the sound will die there. There are only a few notes on the viola that cannot be played on the violin, and they are easily written into the cello part. Some say that letting the violins and celli play the viola notes would change the tone quality. This tone quality can be duplicated by just pushing a heavy chair across the stage.

In the interest of fair reporting, I must tell you three of the many standard riddles that typify the attitude of the orchestra towards the violi.

1. What is the difference between a viola and an onion? Answer. No one cries when you chop up a viola.

2. Which would you choose, a good violist, a bad violist or a pink elephant? Answer. A bad violist. The other two are figments of your imagination.

3. You are a member of the orchestra, and your car is careening down a hill. You must run down either a violist or the conductor. Who do you hit?   Answer. The violist. Business before pleasure.

The String Quartet

The String Quartet combines some of the greatest music ever written with the worst social set-up possible. It has one first violinist, one second violinist, a violist and a cellist. More accurately put, it has a good violinist, a bad violinist, an ex-violinist and a hater of violinists. Actually everyone hates everyone and rehearsals make major surgery look like fun in comparison.

String Quartets change their second violinists like most people change their socks. When the first violinist suspects that the second violinist wants to play loud enough to be heard, he is gone. The violist is second in line to get fired but the replacement is no better.

The cellist stays on for a while until everyone resents his superior attitude. The first violinist stays unless he gets a real job somewhere else. He owns the franchise. Playing in String Quartets is the chief cause of stomach ulcers and colitis in the entire world.

One exception to this rule is the fine musician, Alexander Schneider, who died in 1993. He was the second violinist with the <u>Budapest String Quartet</u> for many years without complaint. If <u>The Second Violinists Hall of Fame</u> is ever completed (or even started) Alexander Schneider should be its most distinguished and only member. There is absolutely no chance that one will ever be built.

I feel the pressure of some strong questions in the air like:

"Aren't some concertmasters really great soloists?"
-

"Aren't the last chair seconds of major orchestras really fine violinists or they would not be in major orchestras?"
-

"Aren't there attractive women cellists who buy flattering concert performance gowns and look and sound wonderful?"
-

"Aren't there fantastic double bassists who can play the violin literature with ease?"
-

"Aren't there violists, considered among the greatest musicians in the world, who concertize using a limited but demanding repertoire?"

Answer:
I consider these queries uncalled for and rude. I will not answer any of them.

Part Two
The Woodwinds

The French Horns

In the middle of the orchestra sit the French horn players... four, five or six, depending on the budget. The members of other sections try to keep as far away as possible. For a while people thought that the great plagues of Europe could be traced to the exact spot where the French horns were seated in the Royal Symphony of London. Even though it has been proven that the plagues preceded the development of these instruments, many still believe that the health disasters started in anticipation of the horns' getting there. The instrument is made up of nine feet of scrunched up small intestines, with removable sections. When the horn player realizes that he sounds like he is playing under water, he removes these pieces of tubing (usually in the middle of the most romantic sections of the music) and empties the contents on the floor. The whole thing is just too disgusting to talk about.

Early French horns had no valves. Each instrument came with twelve replaceable, hollow pretzels of different sizes that allowed the musician to play in all keys. These pieces were called crooks which is the name that most horn players still affectionately call the dealers who sell them their instruments. French horns now come with valves that have eliminated the metal crooks but not the instrument dealers.

Almost everything about the French horns makes very little sense. They are called woodwinds even though the instruments are made entirely of metal and always have been. When a French Horn player sees a C written in the music he plays a C, and calls it a C. Everyone else calls it an F. He plays from music that is written in a different key from everyone else. The chances are that if you ask him what note he is sounding (concert pitch) he will answer with the horn players' motto, "Search me."

If there are six horn players in an orchestra, they are lined up first horn, fifth horn, fourth horn, sixth horn, second horn and third. This is not because French horn players can't count (at least up to six) but because they have convinced orchestra managers that a first horn player only can play high notes and needs an assistant (the fifth horn next to him) so that he won't play too much and blow off the top of his head. The fourth horn player who specializes in the low notes gets an assistant (the sixth horn) in order not to blow off his feet. No one cares a whit about the second and third horn players. It is truly amazing how first horn players manage to play both high notes and low notes when asked to play at recording sessions where they are highly paid. Maybe they consider the extra money hazardous duty pay.

French horn players do most of their practicing at orchestra rehearsals and just before the conductor comes out at concerts. The only thing that they practice is the opening of <u>Till Eulenspiegel</u> by Richard Strauss. This allows them to show once again that some players cannot play both high and low notes.

THIS IS A SERIOUS WARNING. It goes without saying that you never, never invite a French Horn player or Lenny Dykstra [see GLOSSARY] to perform in your home. The result will be the same. No one else will come and you will have to throw out your carpets immediately after the performance.

The Flutes

Almost all flutes are made of silver, but at one time they were wood. There are still a few die-hards who play wooden ones. It has never been proven completely that the sound of the wood flute attracts rats and small children. The flute has a range of about four octaves starting at middle C. The piccolo can go an octave higher and the alto flute can sound a fourth lower.

In order to hold the flute in the approved position, you must keep your right elbow high in the air. Being second flutist in the orchestra is no fun. He must keep reminding the first flutist about the importance of bathing. If the orchestra has the money to afford more than two flutists, then the third flute must remind the second about bathing and so on down the line. Some symphonies give the last flute a little more money because even extra strength underarm deodorants cannot compete against a symphony by Gustav Mahler.

One of the flutists must also be able to play the piccolo. This is called doubling. The piccolo, case and all, can be carried easily in one's pocket. Recording companies and some orchestras pay extra money (cartage) to those who must move very large, heavy instruments to concerts and sessions. Greater than Spiro Agnew's [see GLOS-SARY] running for president or the Queen of England [see GLOSSARY] asking for a handout is the amount of nerve it takes for a second flutist to ask for cartage when he has to bring his piccolo along.

Until about thirty years ago the only woman found in a major orchestra was the harpist. Men harpists did not seem to exist. The first women who managed to break this barrier (other than harpists) were flute players. Symphony orchestra boards decided that female flute players must have names that ended in two vowels, the last of which must be an e, such as Pollee Annie Santae. The boards felt that women with demure names did not cause trouble. They turned out to be wrong when a great flutist with an alias of Susie Roe won an historic court decision (five to four) declaring ability more important than vowels. Susie was allowed to go back to her real name, Julie Baker. Naturally the symphony found a different excuse for firing her when she asked for at least half as much salary as men in her section.

Flute players are probably a little nicer than most members of the woodwinds. You may invite them to play in your home, if you are willing to take the chance that they might play their wooden instruments, and you will have to bring in an exterminator afterwards.

CLARINETS

Clarinets are made of African
Blackwood except for those issued
by the army which are molded out
of one piece of iron. The wooden
instrument is assembled out of
many short sections that fit into
one another. These pieces swell
in hot weather and shrink in the
cold. In order to play in tune the
player must jam his instrument
parts together as tightly as possible in the summer and loosen
them to the point of falling
apart in the winter. There is no way to play
an army clarinet in tune, but, if there is an insur-
rection and the bullets are flying, find an army
band and hide behind the clarinets.

The B-flat clarinet is pitched about an octave
below the flutes. The instrument has a range of
about three octaves. The first two octaves were
perfected in the early nineteenth century. They
are still working on the third.

Like the French horn player, the clarinetist
has no idea what note he is really playing. The

instrument comes in all sizes, and in order not to confuse the player, publishers tailor the notation to the instrument. This means that if a player has learned the notes, clef and fingerings for an A-clarinet, he also can play a little E-flat or a monster bass clarinet using the same fingerings and clef. If he does not have perfect pitch (isn't aware of the real name of the note he is playing) and pays no attention to what the conductor is saying, he is in great shape.

There are two or more clarinets in the symphony orchestra, but not one of them is allowed to use vibrato. They take out their frustrations by doing practical jokes. During breaks they like to sneak around and ink in extra sharps and flats on other people's music. This can waste up to a half hour of rehearsal time.... an hour if they do it to the violas.

When a clarinetist plays in a jazz or dance band he can vibrate himself to pieces, but as a penalty he is expected to double on all sizes of clarinets, saxes and flutes. Although he cannot play any one of them really well, he makes up for it by getting multiple doubling and cartage fees and makes the most money. The drummer, who works the hardest, gets the least.

OBOES AND BASSOONS

The oboes and bassoons are listed together because they have much in common. Both use double reeds to produce the sound. Two pieces of cane called arundo donax, found only in the Var section of southern France (although you may be able to find a little in Vaucluse, if you are really desperate) are shaved and tied together. One end is stuffed into the instrument and the other in the mouth. Learning to make these reeds seems to take a lot more time than learning to play the instruments. If an oboist or bassoonist plays a wrong note in the wrong place in a concert he immediately takes the reed out of the instrument, holds it high in the air and looks at it with great disdain. Everyone now knows that his reed did it. An oboist, as an experiment, tried practicing

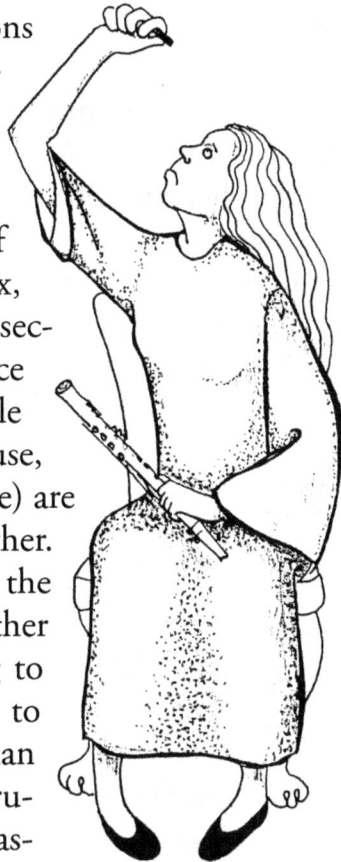

before a concert and was amazed to find out, during the performance, that his reed was pretty good.

During the fifteenth century double reed instruments (early oboes and bassoons) were called rackets. Obviously this name had to be changed. People were saying things like, "Did you hear that racket at the concert last night?" or, "Who made that racket?" when negotiating with instrument dealers. Fifteenth century puns were awful and should not be repeated.

The modern oboe wasn't developed until the nineteenth century and the French oboe, into the twentieth century. It was different in design and sound from the German and Russian instruments. Many historians feel that this lack of standardization was the underlying cause of World War One. After the surrender in a railroad car in France, all countries agreed to use the French fingerings. As far as we know, the Second World War had nothing to do with oboes, although many European countries were irritated when the real spelling of oboe (hautbois) was changed in order to fit into crossword puzzles. The original name for bassoon was dropped in the United States after the First World War when symphony boards decided that the word fagotto sounded dirty.

In <u>The Baseball and Bassoon Players Hall of Fame</u> in Cooperstown, New York there is a bronze statue of Antonio Vivaldi (1675-1741) who wrote over forty concerti for bassoon and orchestra. It is right next to the photograph of Ty Cobb making reeds.

The contra-bassoon was invented by a wood-wind player in Central America who wanted to take over his orchestra by force. Many contra-bassoonists are still on the payroll of the CIA. In the wrong hands the contra-bassoon can sound like an elderly, love-sick moose in distress. In the right hands it sounds pretty much the same. The difference between a bassoon and its bigger brother is about five notes in the bass and a few hundred pounds. Contra-bassoon players get cartage.

The English horn looks like a bent swollen oboe that tried to swallow a tennis ball. It is pitched five notes lower than the oboe and is easier to play. Some rich orchestras employ three oboes and an English horn. In smaller orchestras, oboists fight over who gets to double because great melodic lines are given to the Cor Anglais (English Horn). Some silly people say that the only English horn worth having can be found in a Jaguar sports car.

Experiments prove that the tone quality produced by either a double reed instrument or the human tenor voice destroys the brain cells of the player or singer at a rapid rate. You can prove this to yourself by just trying to have a conversation with a bassoonist. The problem does not seem as pronounced with oboe players, but I am afraid that it is extremely acute with tenors.

You may invite a double reed musician to perform in your home, but do not let him bring his contra-bassoon. It has a naked steel spike to hold it up and it weighs as much as a Buick.

THIS IS A SERIOUS WARNING. Make sure that all double reed players leave after the performance. You do not want to live with one.

Oboe, English horn and bassoon players spend all their time making reeds. They do not see movies, go to shows or eat out. At various times of the day or night they will test out the reeds in progress by blowing into the things. You will be unnerved by this horrible noise. The divorce rate for double reed players is virtually one hundred percent. Tenors, of course, are too busy resonating to get married.

<u>You may ask</u>,
"Isn't there one French horn player that doesn't mess up the stage?"

"Aren't there some flute players who bathe regularly?"

"Aren't there a few musicians on the boards of symphonies?"

"Was there really a Susie Roe who sued a symphony?"

"Isn't there someone who can play an army clarinet in tune?"

"Aren't there a lot of tenors who have not had their brains destroyed?"

"Didn't the CIA stop paying contra-bassoonists a few years back?"

<u>Answer:</u>
Don't count on it.

Part Three
The Brass

The term brass refers to the attitudes of the players more than the metal that makes up these instruments. The brass section has in common one dynamic level, "TOO LOUD," except for the trumpets that have a second setting marked, "LOCKED WHEELS ON AN EXPRESS TRAIN GOING ONE HUNDRED MILES AN HOUR AROUND A CURVE." The players have red rings permanently emblazoned around their lips. A trumpet player gets a little one, the trombonist gets the medium size and the tuba ring goes down to the chin. All three instruments come with the dreaded spit valves. A spit valve, when pressed, allows anything that has accumulated inside the instrument to fall out.

The Tuba

Tuba players try to be as independent and obnoxious as their fellow brass players, but they have some insurmountable problems. They are only employed part time. Many composers forget that the tuba exists, which makes it hard to make a living. When they do work, they seldom play a melodic line, just one or two bass notes per measure. Along with the string bass they share the bottom range of the orchestra. If the instrument is not played absolutely perfectly it sounds like an elephant with severe digestive problems. Some say that, no matter how great the tuba player, there is no cure for that elephant.

An arranger with a warped sense of humor transcribed the piccolo obligato of The Stars And Stripes Forever by John Philip Sousa into a tuba

solo. Once in awhile a sadistic conductor (sorry for the redundancy) will program it into a "Pops Concert" [see GLOSSARY] in order to give everyone a good laugh. This humiliation causes the tuba player to take a drink during the performance. This is known as a tubalibation. Some states want to outlaw both tubalibations and symphonies playing band music.

The tuba is large and awkward to hold. It has so much plumbing in front of the player (eighteen feet squashed into a rectangular shape) that it is difficult for him to see the conductor or the music. A work called Tubby the Tuba is played at Children's Concerts to show that tuba players look just like their instruments.

The band version of the tuba is called a sousaphone. It is designed to make the player look like he is being eaten by a gigantic boa constrictor. The large bell (where the sound comes out) is used primarily as a trash receptacle for the rest of the band.

The Trombone

The nine feet of tubing that make up the trombone have been cleverly arranged so that the spit valve (placed at the very end of the slide) can be emptied into the woodwind section. The trombone is the only instrument in the orchestra that uses a slide to change the pitch.

The only place you can find a valve trombone is in the supply room of an army or navy band. If you own a warehouse full of weird, obsolete instruments that no one has been able to unload since the Civil War, the army will buy them. They will pay any price in order to supply their bands with ridiculous equipment. Besides the usual spiked bass heckelphones and double-belled euphoniums, a military supply room will contain some nice buccina [see Glossary] complete with grotesque dragon's heads and rattling tongues that can be used to scare the enemy. Bullet-proof steel violin bows are available for playing the Brahms Concerto while on the attack.

Although the slide trombone comes in various sizes, from bass to soprano, the tenor or B flat is the one usually used by the two or more players in the symphony. There is, however, only one kind of trombonist found anywhere. His favorite sentence contains six words, "What time do you get off?" He directs this sentence at waitresses, bank tellers, clerks at rental car counters and any other place where women are momentarily stuck with him. He cares not a whit about their size or intelligence or age or appearance or receptiveness. If you are with him, when he is acting his normal self, your skin will creep, but he will not stop. If he ever succeeds in making a date, he feels it will be an incredible moment in history. Some psychiatrists believe that there is something about the way a trombone is played that causes this abhorrent behavior. Other less dirty-minded analysists think that the lecherous personality is attracted to the trombone.

About a year ago, in a documented case in Roanoke, Virginia, a trombonist DID NOT try to make a date with a waitress who had just become a great-great-grandmother. The New York Times decided to do some investigation. It was discovered that the man was an aluminum-siding salesman whose sample case resembled a trombone case. Because he was mistaken for a trombonist, the salesman received many letters of apology. As far as anyone knows, no woman has ever agreed to meet a trombonist after she got off from work.

There is a special place in <u>The National Football League Hall of Fame</u> in Akron, Ohio where a statue exists depicting a man dressed in complete football attire holding a trombone in his hand. The inscription reads, "To the most persistant player of them all (no name given) fifty thousand passes...zero completions."

The Trumpet

Trumpets and trumpet players and the antecedents of trumpets and trumpet players have been irritating the world for thousands of years. In ancient Egypt, Greece and Rome trumpets were used to command and scare the people. Despots had trumpet fanfares signal their arrivals. Even the United States Army used bugles (trumpets without valves) just to be annoying.

Although the modern trumpet was not developed until the early nineteenth century, members of orchestras have been asking trumpet players to pipe down for hundreds of years. In the present day symphony the trumpet's sound is directed toward the viola section knowing that they will have to play with cotton-stuffed ears. If viola players cannot hear their own playing, it lifts their spirits.

The symphony trumpet player uses a C horn with a range similar to the first two octaves of the violin. Jazz trumpeters, not satisfied with this limitation, insist on blowing notes so high and screechy that they should only be heard by dogs and bugs. Unfortunately, this incredible noise can be heard for miles by everyone. Paul Revere could have saved himself a lot of trouble had he only played the trumpet.

Trumpet players are "cool." Cool means always showing up late and saying things like, "What's happening, baby?" Cool means being totally irresponsible with money. Cool means complaining about everything. A trumpet player would never open a window if he felt warm. Instead he would announce, "Hey man, my canary just died."

Because trumpet players are always broke, some aspire to becoming personal money managers or drug dealers. In most state courts, allowing a trumpet player to invest your money is prima-facie evidence of extreme diminished capacity and precocious senility. Only a few trumpet players have made it all the way to drug dealer.

The most peculiar thing about trumpet players is that they keep toilet plungers in their instrument cases. When they hold the rubber end over the bell of the instrument, it makes the trumpet sound like a talking electronic baby duck whose only word is "wawa." It has been impossible to find out why they do this.

Since the trumpet comes with two spit valves, you never invite a trumpet player to perform in your home unless you use a plastic drop cloth, provide earmuffs for your guests and your toilet is stopped up.

Part Four

The Percussion, Harp, Piano and Organ

Bent over two or more kettle drums is the full-time percussionist who is joined by as many other noise-makers as are required for the concert. With one ear on the plastic head (calfskin in the super deluxe model) stretched across the top of the instrument, he devotes his full time to screwing and unscrewing little chromium bars, while tapping with his fuzzy mallet. He is trying to make the kettle-drum sound in tune. We all hope that he makes it some day.

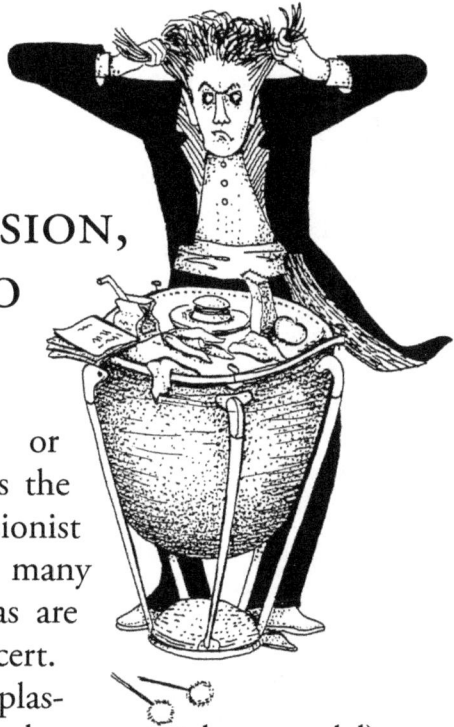

The great frustration of percussionists is that a kettle drum looks like a table. If there is a ten minute break, the percussionist will come back to find that his instrument is covered with magazines, jackets and half-eaten Twinkies. In one instance when a flute was put on a tympany, a tympany was put on a flutist. The case is still in court.

Percussionists are required to play a variety of musical and non-musical instruments. One of these is the glockenspiel which is a group of various sized metal bars that are hit with a hard mallet. These bars are arranged on a metal frame with a rod sticking out the bottom so that it can be held at the waist like a flag. It produces a high, loud, piercing sound that makes it especially useful for bands on parade.

There is just one tiny problem. In order to play the right note you must look at the instrument. Since the glockenspiel is held out to the side while striking it with a mallet, there is no way that the player can look where he is going. Next time you watch a parade look for the glockenspielist. He is the one with a determined look on his face, five feet from the rest of the band, tripping over small children and garbage cans.

The percussionist must also be able to play the xylophone which is a very large glockenspiel with wooden bars arranged like a piano keyboard. It has a range of four octaves. The instrument is mounted on a stand with wheels but never taken on a march. It is played with two or more mallets. The idea for the xylophone originated in Southeast Asia in the fourteenth century and had bars made of bone. No wonder Saint-Saens used it in <u>Danse Macabre</u> to sound like rattling skeletons. The xylophone also resembles a table and is often the repository for trombone cases.

Marimbas appear in Symphony Orchestras but not too often. They resemble the xylophone with additional resonating tailpipes hanging from each pitch. Yearly emissions tests are required in many states. Marimba players are not appreciated in the United States but are national heroes in their native Guatemala. Jerry Lewis is also very popular with Guatemalans, so their opinions are not to be trusted.

The vibraphone is seldom found in the Symphony but is used mostly in jazz combos and dance bands. It was invented in the United States about sixty five years ago so that a marimba could have a vibrato [see Glossary]. At the top of each resonating tailpipe there is a small, round disk that is slowly turned by an electric motor.

Whoever invented this device was in love with the flutter and wow found in bad turntables. Many vibraphone players use as many as six or eight mallets at one time. They figure at least one of them is likely to hit the right note. It is an unwritten law that vibraphone players must grow weird beards.

Looking like a tiny spinet piano is the celesta. It sounds as if a muffled glockenspiel and a half-dozen sugar-plum fairies were stuffed inside. Except for a work by Bela Bartok, the celesta can be played only during the Christmas season.

An elaborate version of the door chimes found in suburban homes is the tubular bells. Sets of chromium tubes up to six or seven feet long are hung from a frame on wheels. The very tops of the tubes are hit with a mallet and are

usually played by a small percussionist on his tip-toes. Without tubular bells the Russians could not have celebrated Napoleon's retreat from Moscow in 1812.

A percussion player must be ready to play the cowbell, which is actually a real cowbell hit with a drumstick. It is hard for dealers to work up more than a one-thousand percent profit on a cowbell. One of Beethoven's greatest errors was in not using cowbells in the <u>Sixth Symphony</u> and then selling them during intermissions stamped, "I was there for the <u>Pastoral</u>". He could have told Waldstein, Kreutzer, Rasumovsky, Kinsky and his other patrons to shove off.

Temple blocks look like smaller and smaller empty wooden Kleenex boxes kept in size place on a stand. When hit with a stick they sound very much like the noise you can make by hitting yourself on the head with your mouth slightly open. They are used quite often to imitate the sounds of midget horses wearing tap shoes galloping across tiny hollow wooden prairies in western music.

Sometimes during Latin American compositions the percussion player must shake his ma-

racas which resemble small bowl-
ing pins that have been stuffed
with something like dried
cockroaches. While us-
ing two of them (one in
each hand), the player
must move his body from
side to side, swing his
shoulders back and forth
and smile incessantly and
knowingly. When play-
ing the castanets, he must
look very serious and stand
tall. Spanish music also re-
quires hitting two sticks, called
claves, together for no appar-
ent reason.

When going to a New
Year's Eve party find a percussionist and ask him if you can
borrow his cabaca, triangle,
slapstick, slide whistle,
ratchet and sleigh bells.
The cabaca is a rattle wrapped in loose bands of
metal that you turn abruptly to make a sliding
noise. The triangle is a chromium bar bent like

a (you guessed it) triangle. It is hung by a string and hit with a small metal stick. The slapstick is comprised of two flat boards that are hinged on one edge and can be slammed like a door. The slide whistle can be purchased at your local Woolworth, although professional percussionists buy the exact same thing through musical instrument specialists for a lot extra. The ratchet is a small cylindrical washboard on a handle with metal or wooden pieces rubbing against it. When the handle is turned, it sounds like someone is holding a stick against a picket fence while running. Fifteen or twenty sleigh bells are attached to a handle and by shaking the sleigh bells they can be made to sound like sleigh bells. So the instrument is called sleigh bells. Sounds simple but a shrewd dealer can work this into a two or three hundred dollar purchase. After all, the professional only wants the best in noisemakers. So after your party, try to bring back the Cabaca, Triangle, Slapstick, Slide Whistle, Ratchet and Sleigh Bells in one piece. They cost a small fortune. Happy New Year!

"They also serve who only stand and wait," is the motto of the percussion section. Like astronauts in space, they experience hours of boredom and busywork interspersed with moments of terror. After counting ninety-two bars of rests, a cymbal player may lose confidence in his arithmetic and look to the conductor for a cue. When he realizes that this is a big mistake, he looks at his fellow percussionists for help. They may be in their own state of panic. There is no faking a cymbal crash. How does he come in right? What is the secret of the percussion section? None. When he blasts off in the wrong place, the orchestra, the audience and sometimes even the conductor know it.

Two popular favorites among percussion players are <u>Konzertstuck</u> (Concert Piece) <u>for Tympany, Piano and Orchestra</u> by Carl Maria von Weber and <u>The Concerto</u> <u>Number Two for Triangle and Piano</u> by Franz Liszt. Weber did not actually include the word tympany in the title and Liszt did not include triangle. Percussion players are positive that these are just accidental omissions.

The complete tympanist must also be prepared to play all kinds of drums including congas, bongos, timbales, snare drums and bass drums. In dance bands, the bass drum is put up on end, facing the audience, with large print advertising across the skin, giving the name of the player, manufacturer, name of the band or any paid advertising the player can get away with.

When employed to play at a country music recording session the tympanist comes with a giant steamer trunk full of all kinds of goodies. Suppose the great creative mind of a record producer discovers it needs the sound of a bag full of damp, dirty sneakers falling into a barrel of pickles to enhance the voice of his delinquent teen-age discovery with the serious throat infection. A fine tympanist is prepared. Damp, dirty, smelly sneakers just about describe the great, creative mind of the country-music record producer.

There are small orchestras made up exclusively of percussion instruments called percussion ensembles. The audience for this type of group is made up mostly of drummers. There is actually a repertoire for percussion ensembles. If you attend such a concert, you will find your fascination lies somewhere between seeing the Tennessee Walking Horse Show and a sales pitch on life insurance. If you can get the ensemble to perform in your home, your neighbors will think that Amtrak sent a train through your living room.

The Harp

A harp has forty seven strings and seven foot pedals. Each pedal has three positions allowing the entire instrument to be put into a variety of chords. Does this mean that it should be played by a man or a woman? For thousands of years harpists were men until World War I when an American general decided that playing the harp was cause for immediate dismissal from the army. He came to that conclusion after realizing that harpists do not use their pinkies but leave them suspended in the air. The son of that general buys instruments for military bands.

Since that time most harpists in the United States have been women. The notable exception was Harpo Marx, who was allowed to play the harp in the movies after he agreed not to say a word about it. In parts of Africa and South America a woman found playing a harp can be executed or made to sit through the last quartets of Arnold Schoenberg.

Harpists, like tuba players, are only part-time members of the orchestra and have very low incomes. This causes them to pocket the money they have been given for having the harp moved to rehearsals and concerts. Instead, they bring it themselves. Since the harp weighs almost as much as a small piano, the harpist must have help getting it out of her van and onto the stage. She can not ask anyone from the orchestra administration. Her moving expenses have been paid. Other musicians will help out for awhile, but, after a few bouts carrying harps up staircases and through doorways, members of the orchestra jump into closets if they see a harpist approaching. In an emergency she can always count on a trombonist for help, but it may not be worth it. In the Harpists' Hall of Fame in Elmira, New York, there is a special section for composers who have given work to harpists.

Especially popular are Berlioz, Liszt and the French Impressionists. Most cherished of all is Wagner, who scored <u>Das Rheingold</u> for seven harps. High above his picture is the haunting inscription, "We who pick, love you Dick."

THE PIANO

Most pianists are considered the orphans of music and those who are members of orchestras are treated like unnecessary evils. There are less than a few dozen pianists in the country who make a good living as piano soloists and just three or four of those get to travel with their own instruments. Vladimir Horowitz took his piano, his wife (Toscanini's daughter) and his cook with him to every concert he played.

These thirty-six or so special soloists are treated with great respect, are well paid and play on the best instruments made. The other

100,000 pianists are trying to establish themselves. They keep from starving by touring alone or with chamber groups, accompanying violinists, cellists and singers, providing background music at parties, playing in restaurants or working in orchestras as one of the musicians. From here on we refer to them.

The modern piano has eighty-eight keys, two or three pedals (loud, soft and sustaining) and a touchy system made up of at least thirty-five parts for each note. Added together that makes over three thousand things to go wrong in the action alone. Any one of these parts not working correctly can make a pianist's life miserable.

When away from home, all instrumentalists may have to put up with uncomfortable chairs, cold or overheated halls, bad food, non-existent lighting and have to deal with total incompetents or even musicologists. But when they play they have the security of their own familiar instruments. Being a pianist comes with most of those problems plus a recurring nightmare. That nightmare is the surprise pile of junk waiting for the pianist at a local job (gig) or out-of-town concert.

There it is, a very low iron patio chair with arms as a piano bench and a La Farge upright sold by Sears in 1910 with thumb tacks in the hammers for a piano. The old ivory keys are so worn that they have become razor thin and just as sharp. Some of the edges look as if they were cut with pinking shears. The last time it was tuned was during the Hoover administration.

The keyboard has several types of notes. Some go down but do not want to come back up and some do come up but make no sound when pushed down. Several seem to be glued to other keys. A few notes have mysteriously missing dampers so the only way to stop the continuing sound is by throwing your arm into the piano. On some of the notes all that is left is the remains of the glue that once held the ivory on the keys.

Of course the peg that holds up the lid is missing and the white keys have turned yellowish black and the black keys have faded to a whitish yellow. Add to that a thick layer of grime that multiplies the difficulty of telling one key from another. Only one pedal is working and it creaks and moans. It is waiting for the middle of the concert to fall off. You find yourself with a page turner who, because he does not read music, is looking for his girlfriend in the audience while you are playing some of the more difficult passages. No amount of pleading can get his attention when the page needs turning.

When music-hating roaches come out between the high A and B flat to see who is playing, the nightmare is complete. How frequently does this nightmare turn out to be real? Very frequently.

The worst thing is that the pianist knows he must do everything for himself. Even if he or she is part of an ensemble or orchestra, the pianist still feels deserted. No one else seems to care. Pianists are famous for complaining, and other musicians are immune to it.

How do you cope? You come hours before the rehearsal or concert and give up having dinner. You use the time to tape the edges of the keys so as not to cut your hands to pieces. You do a certain amount of repairs and tune up some of the worst notes. You find an open office and borrow a chair that comes closest to being the right height and add telephone books if necessary. While in the office you remove someone's desk lamp and with the fifty-foot extension cord you have brought from home, you plug it into some far away socket. You balance the lamp on the piano wherever possible. You use a dictionary to hold up the lid and carry insect spray, paper towels and grease cleaner. Then you practice the music in a way that will allow you to avoid some of the horrors of the instrument.

When the concert is over, even if you have just played on a piano that was only good as a buoy for the QE2 or are covered with your own blood because the piano legs have broken off and it has crashed to the ground almost killing you, smile and talk about something else. No one cares. You are on your own.

Pianists, who are members of the Symphony Orchestra, play in less than half the concerts. They are offered and usually accept contracts for forty percent of the bottom full-time salary. They will accept it because there are hundreds of pianists for every job, and symphony orchestras that rehearse in established concert halls usually have decent pianos. But then the trouble begins.

When one of the three dozen established solo pianists is invited to perform with an orchestra, he or she is put in an honored place at the edge of the stage, next to the conductor and enters the concert to the applause of the audience. The pianist, who is a member of the orchestra, is squeezed into a space between the second violins and the percussion section.

Often at the beginning of a rehearsal but after the entire orchestra is seated, those who set up the orchestra remember that the piano is needed as part of the percussion section. Almost everyone must move as the piano is rolled onto the stage to its place behind the seconds. You can hear the groaning and complaining everywhere. Who is to be blamed for this foul-up? Obviously the piano player. "It sure was nice before she got here." The librarian realizes that he has forgotten to bring the piano part. How can you be expected to remember about piano players? Everyone glares at the pianist who stopped the rehearsal because she forgot her music and piano.

Not that the pianist is blameless. Because pianists are not accustomed to working with other musicians they can not count up the tacit measures (rests) when they play as part of an orchestra. The spaces drive them crazy. A pianist coming in at the correct place in a rehearsal would even shock the viola players.

When there is finally a piano and music, the rehearsal begins. Immediately the second violinists start complaining that the piano is too loud. They want a sound barrier called a baffle between them and the piano. With this baffle it may no longer be too loud for the second violins but most of the audience will never hear a note the pianist is playing or be aware that she is on the stage.

In the not-so-rich professional symphony (that includes most) the orchestra pianist, when she is not busy at her instrument, may find herself called upon to play the celesta, gong or any other instrument that will allow the orchestra to hire one less percussionist. Rushing from place to place, playing a variety of instruments, and trying to remember where you are in the music can be a harrowing experience. If the orchestral management is too cheap to hire a harpist, the orchestra's pianist will get to play the harp part on the piano.

If a harpsichord, the forerunner of the piano used in music from the sixteenth to eighteenth centuries, is required, chances are the pianist will get that assignment too. During a Pops Concert, the orchestral pianist may be called upon to play in a jazz combo or shake her maracas with the right expression on her face.

Some of the most extensive orchestral piano parts that are found in the twentieth century literature were written by Saint-Saens, Ravel, Stravinsky, Prokofief, Bartok, Mahler, Bernstein and Copland. It is interesting that when Bartok wrote The Concerto for Orchestra he featured every section but left out the piano.

Obviously the greatest piano works with orchestra are concerti written by Mozart, Beethoven, Brahms, etc. They are not performed by the regular orchestra pianists unless they are filling in during rehearsals until the soloists get there. Sometimes, in The Carnival of Animals by Saint-Saens, the orchestra pianist is allowed to play one of the two solo piano parts in the concert. This is her big moment. She sits in front of the orchestra, and the second violins are not allowed to complain. Of course Saint-Saens has given both pianists beginner exercises to play and calls them animals.

Pianists have great self-confidence and think

they know everything until they join an orchestra. They are practically the only instrumentalist that sees the entire picture while practicing. They play both the melody and the harmony at the same time. When working as part of an orchestra, it comes as a complete shock when they realize that the music continues while they are not playing. Trying to count these empty bars, playing strange assortments of percussion instruments, finding their rightful place on the stage and arguing with the second violins eventually makes orchestral pianists abrasive and crazy.

Women concert pianists wear beautiful and stylish outfits. Women orchestral pianists tend to buy used parachute dresses after the cellists are finished with them, especially if those gowns become exceptionally seedy. Bass players like to marry these pianists. As a couple, they set a minimum standard in formal wear for the orchestra.

Most piano players like to give joint recitals with themselves. They grunt, they groan, they hum, they sing and they make faces like they were being tortured. All this to the accompaniment of the piano. Putting your forehead on the keyboard with your elbows high in the air and touching a key as if it were white hot is the norm.

Trying to make the note vibrate (an impossibility) while looking passionately at the ceiling all goes with your love for the piano. Love for the piano and teaching twenty reluctant ten-year-olds on Saturdays and after school will keep you barely eating.

THIS IS A SERIOUS WARNING. When you are introduced to a pianist at a party, do not say, "Oh, so you're the one who tickles the ivories." At best, your conversation will end right there.

THE ORGAN

The three orchestral works famous for using the organ are <u>The Planets</u> by Gustav Holst, <u>Symphony Number Three</u> by Camille Saint-Saens and <u>The Alpine Symphony</u> by Richard Strauss. There are a few other orchestral pieces that call for an organ. Most of the time, there is no organ in the hall, and the part is played on the piano. If the pianist has to play the organ, she makes believe she knows how the registers work and forgets about the foot pedals. Chances are it will sound a lot better than if an organist were hired.

SHELDON KURLAND   63

Organists are the violists of the keyboard instruments. Most of them are dropout pianists.
Naturally the major instrument of musicologists
is the organ. Organists like to play everything
at half speed because this is as fast as they can
go. The most horrible experience a violinist can
have is being accompanied by an organist. The
slow, boring, loud, droning noises coming out
of the organ can be truly depressing.

When the organist tries to play cheerful music, the listener thinks that somebody must have
died. It was clever of Saint-Saens in his <u>Organ
Symphony</u> to change the the scoring in order
to keep the music from moving at a snail's pace.
At first he wrote the symphony without piano
parts but he quickly saw the light. He edited out
most of the organ part after the first rehearsal.
He changed it to give all the difficult keyboard
parts to two pianists. He should have re-named
the work, <u>Symphony Number Three for Two
Pianos and a Little Bit of Organ</u>

Many organists work in churches where
they are responsible for making the services last
so long. Do I hear you yelling, "Wasn't Bach a
church organist and composer of great organ
music?" Yes, he did write great music for the or-

gan and have a church job but for all we know he played very slowly and was doing it to get out of the house.

Dietrich Buxtehude, Cesar Franck and Max Reger, among others, wrote volumes of music for the organ. Why do they all sound the same when you listen to them? Because everything seems to be played at the same dragging tempo in weird registers. There is nothing more disconcerting than turning on the radio on a Sunday morning hoping to hear a beautiful Mozart String Quartet or a Trio by Schubert and being inundated by this awful collection of loud, slow, dreary hot air noises from some church service.

There are two kinds of organs, The first is the pipe organ found in cathedrals, concert halls, Radio City Music Hall and some very old department stores. The other kind is electric. Some think that a third type, the electronic synthesizer [see [see Glossary]], sounds peculiar enough to be called an organ. When an organ is scored into an orchestral work everyone must tune to that organ. In some halls the built in organ's pitch is so flat that it cannot be fixed. It is impossible to bring in another instrument. Pipe organ-transplants have not been perfected. If the organ is being played by the orchestra pianist, everyone will agree that the poor intonation (tuning) is her fault.

When organists play away from their home instrument, they have the same problems as pianists. Most organs are in terrible shape. Before Albert Schweitzer became a medical missionary in Africa, he played organ concerts all over Europe. He discovered that he had to get to each concert a day or two early to reconstruct and tune each instrument. As his popularity and engagements grew, he discovered that institutions wanted his services because he fixed their organs. His concert honorarium was much lower than the fee of an organ repairman.

After the realization of why he was hired, he almost threw a low fourteen foot B flat pipe that was in awful shape through a stained glass window of a church. At the last possible moment, he remembered he was ALBERT SCHWEITZER and finished fixing the instrument. Even while doing his work in Africa, he came back to Europe occasionally to give lecture-concerts but had the organs scouted in advance.

PART FIVE

THE SAXOPHONE AND OTHER STRANGE THINGS LIKE THE CONDUCTOR

You may also see a saxophone show up in the orchestra in some twentieth century work, usually in French Impressionist music. The sax comes in seven sizes. The one with the highest pitch is the sopranino which is sent in an hour before the concert to scare the bugs out of the hall. It should never be used in front of an audience. The largest is the contra-bass Sax which may exist in theory only. There is also a bass sax. Most common are the soprano, alto, tenor and baritone saxes.

Everyone thinks of the sax as an American instrument but it was invented in France by a man born in Brussels. An American saxophone player named Boots Randolph calls himself "Mr. Sax" but the real Mr. Sax was Adolphe Sax (the inventor) who died in 1894. Is it possible that when Adolph was on tour in France he called himself Mr. Randolph?

OTHER INSTRUMENTS

Anvils are written into opera orchestras scores by Wagner and Verdi. It is also a possibility that you will see flugelhorns (funny looking trumpets used mostly in bands), sackbuts (even funnier looking trombones), recorders, and every kind of percussion noisemaker a modern composer may demand. George Antheil scored his <u>Ballet Mecanique</u> for air-hammer (road drill) and airplane engine with propeller. He had to remove the propeller when he blew the front doors off Carnegie Hall. What you will not find are sweet potatoes, ocarinas, harmonicas, banjos, accordions, cannons or whistling alligators, unless you are at a Park Concert.

THE CONDUCTOR

First-rate instrumental soloists and members of the orchestra make fine conductors. They know the importance of a precise beat, clear cues, good use of rehearsal time and communicating the music to the audience. Because of their interest in quality and their disinterest in histrionics, they are disasters to those who worry about symphony attendance. The really great conductor, by symphony board standards, is involved with the things that do count. The most important qualities are a haircut that looks good from the back, designer tails, a good press agent and compelling choreography.

Arturo Toscanini, "World's Greatest Conductor", never had a press release that did not have the words "world's greatest conductor" after his name. When he was with the NBC Symphony, you could always find cute little stories in papers like the New York Post that said, "Arturo Toscanini, world's greatest conductor, fired two flutists and a violist the day before Christmas when he discovered they did not like pasta." The broadcasting executives realized they had overdone it when publicity like this made Toscanini so powerful that NBC had to wait until he retired before dismantling the orchestra.

Leopold Stokowski was famous for many accomplishments besides his wonderful hair. His greatest was getting married to Gloria Vanderbilt and becoming a father while in his seventies. Shortly after his marriage he made a movie called Music For Millions. He conducted without a baton and scored some Bach organ Preludes and Fugues for slide trombones and orchestra. It is for these reasons Stokowski is in the Trombone Players Hall of Fame which is located between the Hertz and Avis counters at the Houston airport. His detractors say putting trombones in a Bach fugue is like playing ping-pong with a cannonball. Others say Stokowski detractors are musical snobs.

His least famous accomplishment was in the great number of musicians he fired. Stokowski was musical director of the Cincinnati, Philadelphia and New York orchestras when unions were weak and musicians were even more desperate than they are now. People were tossed out with such regularity that musicians were afraid to tell him that it was time for the contracted lunch break or that the time had run out. If they did, they were gone. Rehearsals lasted indefinitely.

Sometimes if they were on tour and too many people were fired, the personnel manager, if he could not come up with good new players, would sneak the original people back into the orchestra in disguises. No matter how bitterly the musicians complained about him, they had to admit that he was nice to Deanna Durbin in the movie, <u>One Hundred Men and a Girl</u>. The one hundred men were The Philadelphia Orchestra. I guess they did not count the harpist. <u>Ninety-nine Men and a Woman and a Girl</u> would have made a poor title.

One of the most lop-sided races in the history of the orchestra occurred between Thor Johnson conductor of the <u>Cincinnati Symphony</u> and Oscar Levant the guest soloist. The music was the <u>Concerto in F</u> by George Gershwin.

Mr. Levant decided not to bother coming for the planned rehearsal and arrived just a few minutes before the sold-out concert. He was now a big (for a piano player) movie star and he felt that he had rehearsed Gershwin's music enough for one lifetime. Oscar had been a buddy of George Gershwin and Gershwin was the only composer that orchestras wanted him to play. He told Thor, " We don't need a rehearsal. Just listen and watch and you won't have trouble following me. Haven't you heard my recording?" Thor Johnson was livid.

Conductors are supposed to follow the soloists no matter what they do, but Thor decided to teach Levant a lesson. He started at a lively tempo and then very gradually slowed down. Levant tried to speed things up by conducting with one hand and playing with the other. He called to Thor who looked the other way. Thor would not be moved. At first a few players followed Levant and there was chaos. A few dirty looks from Thor and all of the members of the orchestra thought it was in their best interest to follow their regular leader. Oscar was forced to play at Thor's tempo.

Halfway through the last movement Oscar had enough. He stood up and yelled comments to the audience and instructions to the orchestra. He desperately tried to urge them on. Thor was not intimidated. He slowed down to a crawl. The one-sided race was on. Oscar decided to go his merry way. He finished a full minute and a half ahead of <u>The Cincinnati Symphony</u>. He even had time to sip some coffee (which he kept on the piano) and tell a joke, before the orchestra pulled into the station.

A conference was arranged between the two the next day and some kind of detente was achieved, or so they thought. For some reason no rehearsal was held before the second performance (a big mistake). This time Oscar Levant took off even earlier and finished over three minutes before the orchestra, establishing a new mark which will be hard to beat. Oscar never came back to Cincinnati and, at the end of his contract Thor Johnson moved to, what was then, a semi-professional orchestra in Nashville.

Yes, for those of you who keep insisting, I will admit that Leonard Bernstein was not only a conductor who was appreciated by the members of The New York Philharmonic but was a good composer and pianist as well. His fame brought recording sessions and world tours to an orchestra whose audiences were diminishing and whose reputation was disappearing before he got there. The best score ever written for a musical on Broadway has to be his West Side Story. Of course, best music on Broadway is not much of an accomplishment. As a lovable conductor Leonard Bernstein may have been an aberration in music history.

Perhaps many conductors have not been given a fair chance. Once, when a guest conductor at a major orchestra arrived at the podium for the first time and said, "Good morning" to the musicians, one violinist was overheard saying to his stand-partner, "I hate his guts already."

If Beethoven was hired to be permanent conductor of a present-day symphony (a good trick), everyone in the orchestra, symphony society and audience would be thrilled. The orchestra would have a great first season. During the second year the symphony board would complain that Ludwig did not want to come to all the social events and was sort of unpleasant at the few he attended. During the third year the audience would protest that he was programming "an awful lot of his own music", and the musicians would be mumbling about him having such a terrible accent and going deaf. At the end of the fourth year everyone would be glad to see him go and have high hopes for Mozart, the new man.

From Greek tablets dating back over two thousand years we learn that the weakest member of a music ensemble was given a wood pole to move up and down in time to the music in order to get him to stop playing. In later writings we discover that the pole was taken away in order to stop him from being a know-it-all. He was then allowed to stamp his foot.

Foot-stamping and the conducting pole were used to keep the incompetent from playing for the next fifteen hundred years until Bartolomeo Ramos de Pereia was allowed to use a gesturing hand. His hand was eventually cut off when all of Rome felt that they had created a monster. The first conductors who were allowed to use their hands were all well known composers performing their own music. Among them we find the names of Berlioz and Wagner who, as we know, both made the Harpists' Hall of Fame.

Berlioz, however, lost the respect of most musicians when he wrote an essay entitled, <u>Conductors? Are they really that bad?</u>

Carl Maria von Weber (composer of <u>Conzertstuck</u>) was the first full-time conductor with an expensive haircut. Some say he was described by Sigmund Freud as a "paranoiac defending himself with a stick." Freud also discovered that just owning a baton was enough to turn one into a galloping egomaniac. Students of Freud, continuing his great work, announced at a turn-of-the-century symposium in Vienna, "Waving a piece of wood in front of an orchestra makes you irritable, sarcastic, power crazy and delusional. Conductors actually believe that the sounds are coming out of their batons." No other study has ever refuted this statement.

There is a present-day school of conducting that believes that exposing the beat to the orchestra is like giving away the nation's secrets. Chief exponent of this theory was the great William Steinberg, Musical Director of the Pittsburgh Symphony. The Yale University Music School considered offering one year's free tuition to anyone who could figure out what he was doing. Some felt that anyone who could

find Steinberg's beat should be given a Doctor-
ate. The orchestra survived. It has been proven
that, musically, no conductor at all works best.

So if your skin is thick, your ego is the size
of Asia, can't play any instrument too well, you
have great hair, own tails and are prepared to tell
a group of one hundred virtuosi that you want
the first 20 measures to sound like little pink
elves, dancing on their tippy-toes while a multi-
colored sun slowly rises, you might think about
becoming Musical Director of a great orchestra.

In the electronic era a flashy conductor is a
necessity. What would the audience watch? Not
the strings who do nothing better than go up
and down at the same time. Not the woodwinds
who spend their time looking at their reeds with
disgust. Not the brass who are always emptying
their spit valves. You can't even turn a knob for
more bass, change the balance or put the discs in
a different order. That conductor better put on
a good show. After all, while you are watching
the back of his beautiful hair bouncing on his
custom-made jacket, your car is on a hook being
towed off to the pound.

Here are questions that people insist I answer.

"Why are you so hard on conductors?"

Answer: No harder than they are on themselves. The composer Jean Baptiste Lully, in a great passion, desperately trying to find the beat, brought his big conducting stick down on his foot and gave himself blood poisoning. He died a few days later on March 22, 1687

-

"Surely not all trombonists are womanizers, are they?"

Answer: You are right. A small percentage are manizers.

-

"Isn't there a piece of music where you think the trumpet isn't too loud, and aren't there people who like the trumpet?"

Answer: Yes. In the <u>Leonora Overture Number Three</u> Beethoven had the good sense to put the trumpet player offstage in a soundproof room by himself. However, I must admit that the A-HAM-A* gives its full support to all trumpet players.

-

"Are all tuba players heavy drinkers?"

Answer: No, a few have taken off weight.

---

* American Hearing Aid Manufacturers Association

"Don't you think you are going too far when
don't show respect for Arturo Toscanini and
William Steinberg? Next thing you will say
is that Pablo Casals was a lousy conductor."
Answer: Pablo Casals was a lousy conductor.
-

Is there a statute of limitations on sacred cows?
Answer: I am about to find out.......

Glossary of Orchestral Terms

Acoustics
The science of selling the Emperor his new clothes.

Adagio
Tempo played by organists when they see the word presto.

Army Band
One hundred or more soldiers play <u>The Syncopated Clock</u> by Leroy Anderson in a desperate attempt to stay out of the infantry.

Assistant Conductor
Conductor of Children's Concerts, Pop Concerts, Benefit Concerts, Park Concerts and any road performances reached by bus.

Ballet Orchestra
It is the same set-up as the Opera Orchestra except that the musicians only hear the thumping and banging coming from the dancers on the stage, instead of the thumping, banging and singing that you get from the sopranos.

Benefit Concert
Big stars work for expenses and a small honorarium. After paying for limousines, hotel suites, midnight suppers, first class air fares and the small (only by Hollywood standards) honorarium the charity is lucky if they have money left to file bankruptcy.

Buccina
Incredibly expensive curved imaginary trumpets dating from the Roman Empire. It can only be found in ancient writings and army band supply rooms. It is used to cheer up the enemy and fleece the taxpayers.

Children's Concert
Bedlam with Peter and the Wolf as background music.

Classical Period
Music from about 1750 to 1840. To some it means any music without an electric guitar and drum.

Concert Hall
Auditorium in the no-parking section of town where you can buy watery lemonade at a price that makes movie popcorn look like a steal.

Crwth
A violin from the middle ages that could not play the notes A, E, I, O, or U

Do you play classical or popular?
One of the most irritating questions you can ask a musician.

Electronic Synthesizer
A modern device that can make over ten thousand different kinds of sounds, all horrible.

Guest Conductor
Conductor who is making extra money in another city while his own orchestra is playing a Park Concert.

Harmonics
A string player takes advantage of the overtone series by putting his fingers lightly on the string so as to imitate a gas leak or someone blowing over the top of a very small bottle. Very high harmonics are found in the opening of The Rite of Spring by Igor Stravinsky.

Double Harmonics
A violinist puts in years of practice so he can produce two gas leaks in harmony in order to impress other violinists. It makes non-violinists sick to their stomachs.

High School Orchestra
An experiment by scientists to show that time is relative. One rehearsal of a high school orchestra seems to be the equivalent of the Hundred Years War.

Humoresque
A light, romantic piece from the nineteenth century. Also a movie where a violinist's career is saved when Joan Crawford walks into the Pacific Ocean. It is unfortunate that she did not take the rest of the film with her.

Intermezzo
Short piano pieces by Schumann and Brahms. Also a movie where a very successful violinist gives up his career, his wife, his children and everything else to be with Ingrid Bergman when she was twenty-one. Naturally.

Lenny Dykstra
Major league baseball player most prolific in chewing tobacco and spitting disgusting, brown juice. When last seen he was the center fielder and musicologist for the Philadelphia Phillies.

Mute
A device used by an instrumentalist while practicing in order not to break his lease. Occasionally it is utilized in concerts. In Finland, because of its close proximity to the North Pole, head-

lights on cars must be kept on at all times and mutes must be permanently attached to trumpets to avoid avalanches.

Monotone
Person with no sense of pitch, sometimes referred to as a Musicologist.

Musicologist
A person who is thrilled by a dreary performance played on bad instruments.

Opera Orchestra
A small orchestra in a dirty trench called a pit between an opera company and the audience. A conductor stands in front of the orchestra and waves frantically with his baton, while he tries to figure out where the singer has jumped to in the score. During Wagner operas, emergency food, water, and medicine are thrown into the pit by the United Nations.

Pops Concert
A large symphony orchestra turns show-tunes

into hundred ton weights and very slowly drags
them across the stage

Park Concert
A Pops Concert, with insects and rain, using
an amplification system rescued from a 1938
Dodge.

Program Notes
Total nonsense taken off the back of a record
jacket.

Queen of England
One of the richest women in the world and
head of the British royal family. All her children
turned out to be trombone players.

Reception for the Artist
A great musician and performer is forced by the
terms of his contract to have dinner with members of the Symphony Board who ask him, "How
long have you been taking piano?" or, "What do
you really do for a living?"

Rhapsody
Instrumental music of the nineteenth and twentieth centuries, sometimes heroic or nationalistic, written by Bartok, Liszt, Brahms, Lalo, Gershwin and others. Also a movie where a violinist turns down the advances of eighteen-year-old Elizabeth Taylor in order to practice. It gives a new demention to the word, fiction.

Slow Movement
Second movement of a symphony from the classical period where an entire audience suddenly discovers that it has tuberculosis.

Spiro Agnew
Former Vice President during the Nixon administration who was removed from office after it was discovered that he was selling the names and phone numbers of women White House employees to trombone players.

Symphony Board
A group of up to one hundred people who wear very serious suits and dresses to meetings, know absolutely nothing about music and have (or

their spouses have) scads of money. The night-mare of any orchestral association is that the board would actually make policy. The real object of being on a symphony board is that you can say, "I am on the Symphony Board", to people at the country club. It makes you sound highly intellectual. The real reason that you have been put on the board is that you are expected to donate many bucks and buy season tickets for yourself and your symphony bored loved one.

TicketScam *(Comes under a variety of names)*
The place you can call or go to for concert reservations providing that you have the patience of a saint, enjoy paying extra and don't care where you sit. If there is one person in line ahead of you, be sure your whole day is free.

Twelve-tone Music
A twentieth century system of composition, sometimes referred to as Serial Music, that tries to eliminate all traces of traditional melody, harmony and audience.

University Marching Band
College students, in costumes designed by the King of Prussia, teach the football players how to read by spelling out words with their bodies during half-time.

Vibrato
A slight movement of pitch alternating up and down to enhance the quality of the sound. String players move their fingers, wind players change their armatures and singers have their own systems. If the vibrato is too wide, the real pitch disappears. People give Bert Lahr (The Cowardly Lion) credit for having the most extreme vibrato. Obviously those people have not heard some of the famous opera stars lately.

Waltz King and Other Kings
Richard Strauss got tired of telling society women who were "just thrilled to meet the Waltz King", that he was not the composer of the Blue Danube. Johann Strauss, both father and son, had died in the nineteenth century. In self-defense Richard composed some of the most beautiful waltzes ever written for the opera Der Rosenkavalier in 1911. After the debut of

his opera he modestly admitted that, yes, he was now The King. The title was passed on to Elvis Presley. He was a singer who was careful not to allow elements of good taste to seep in and ruin his performances. Since his death Elvis has been spotted quite frequently at the Mozart Festivals in Salzburg.

Every fact in this guide has been verified by at least two of the following sauces:

Paul Newman's Industrial Strength Spaghetti, Heinz Tomato, Franco American Cheese, Kroger's Light and the Oxford Dictionary of Music.

I would also like to thank H.R.(trombone), G.C.(trumpet), S.L.(symphony board member), S.P.(violist), W.K.(daughter of a great violinist) C.H. and E.K. (pianists) and the many wonderful folks who work in symphony orchestras.

www.ingramcontent.com/pod-product-compliance
Lightning Source LLC
Chambersburg PA
CBHW062006040426
42447CB00010B/1943